I CAN DRAW

CHRISTMAS
BY TONY TALLARICO

Little Simon

Published by Simon & Schuster Inc., New York

THIS BOOK IS DEDICATED TO:
Santa's eight tiny reindeer and
especially to you,

Little Simon
Simon & Schuster Building
Rockefeller Center
1230 Avenue of the Americas
New York, New York 10020

Copyright © 1990 by Anthony Tallarico

LITTLE SIMON and colophon are trademarks
of Simon & Schuster Inc.

Manufactured in the United States of America

10 9 8 7 6 5 4 3 2 1

ISBN: 0-671-70446-X

Begin by drawing the first two steps lightly in pencil. Don't be surprised if you have to erase a lot, but always make your corrections and additions before erasing your mistakes.

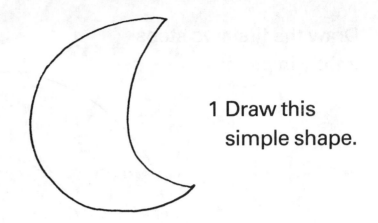

1 Draw this simple shape.

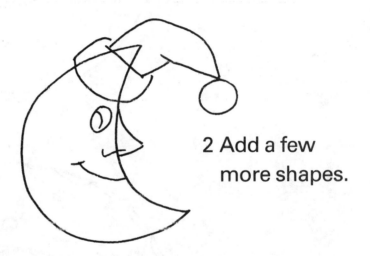

2 Add a few more shapes.

3 Erase the guidelines and complete the drawing with details.

CHRISTMAS MOON

Draw the first two steps lightly in pencil.

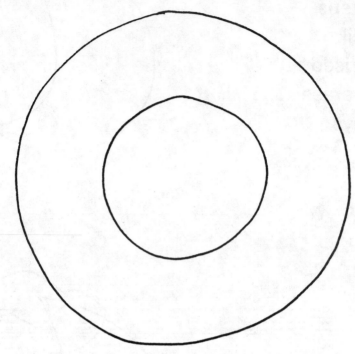

1

2

Erase the guidelines and
add details.

3

CHRISTMAS WREATH

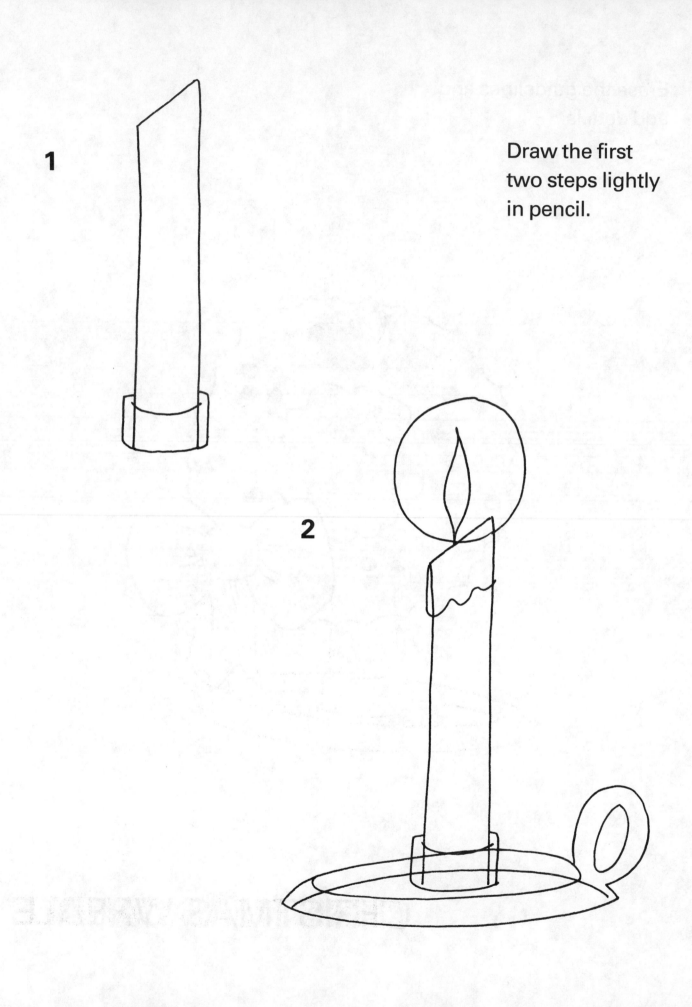

1

Draw the first
two steps lightly
in pencil.

2

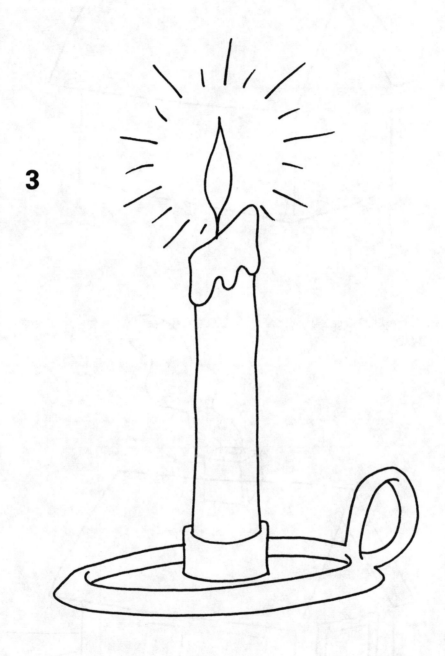

3

CHRISTMAS CANDLE

Draw the first
two steps lightly
in pencil.

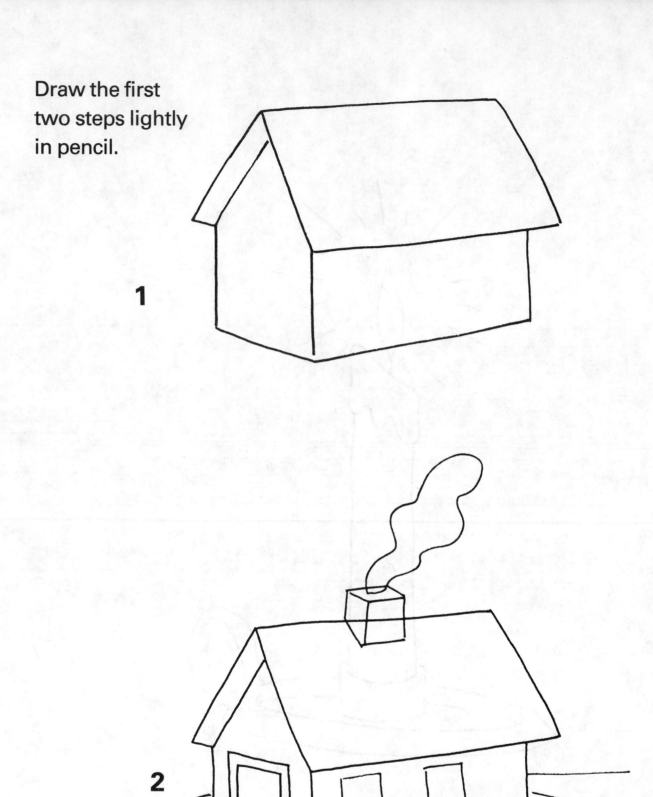

1

2

3

SNOWFALL

1

2

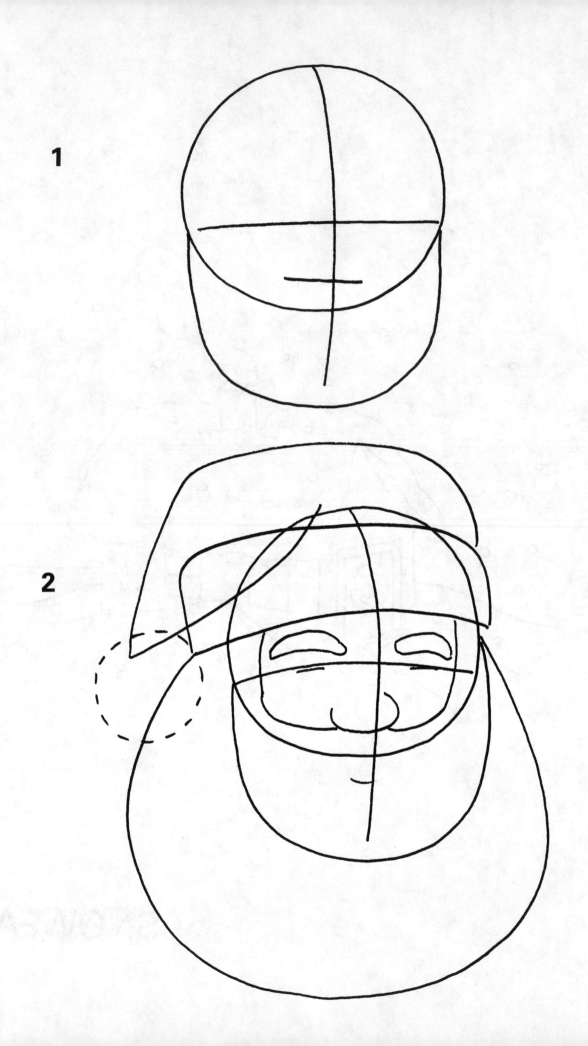

3

SANTA CLAUS

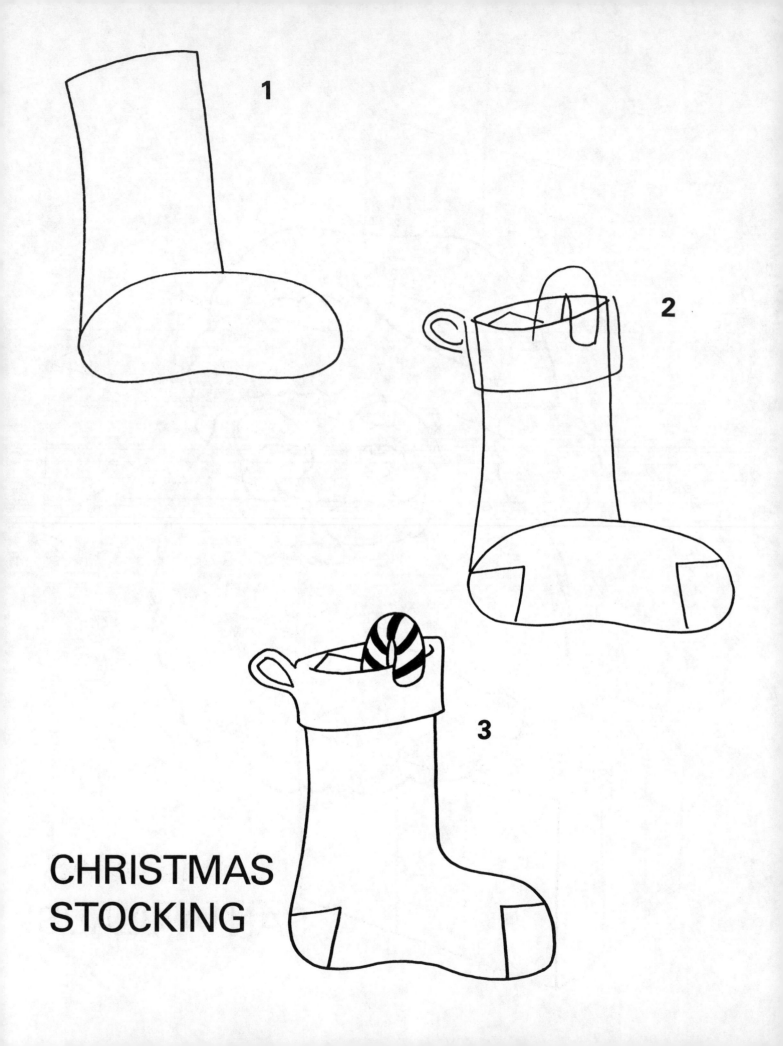

1

2

3

CHRISTMAS
STOCKING

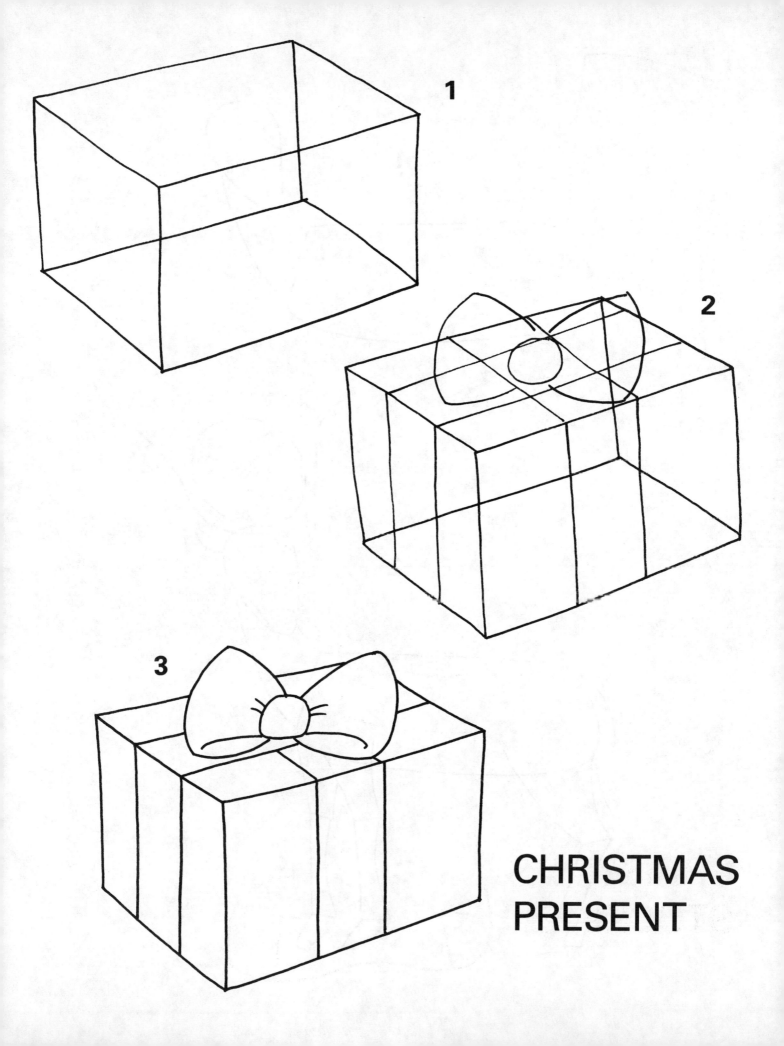

1

2

3

CHRISTMAS
PRESENT

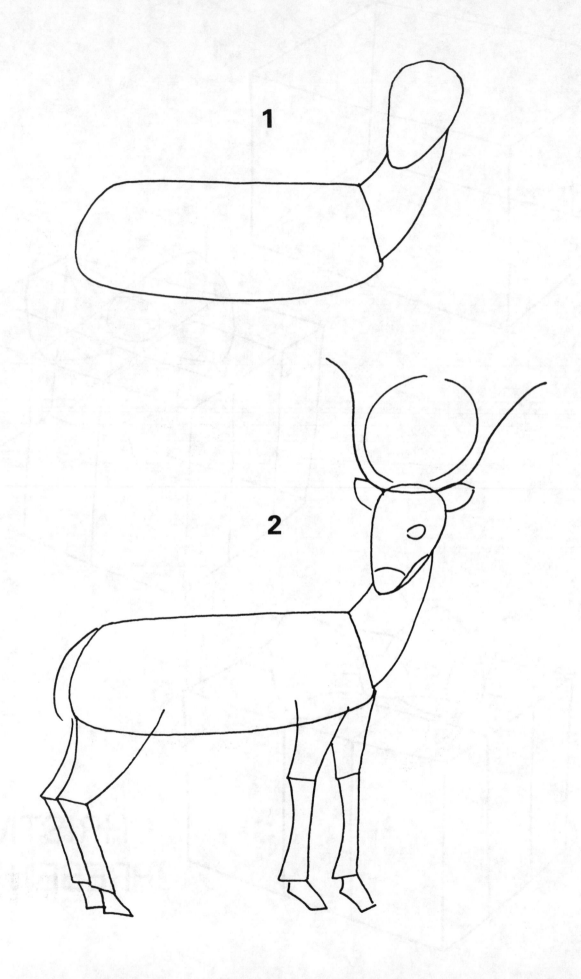

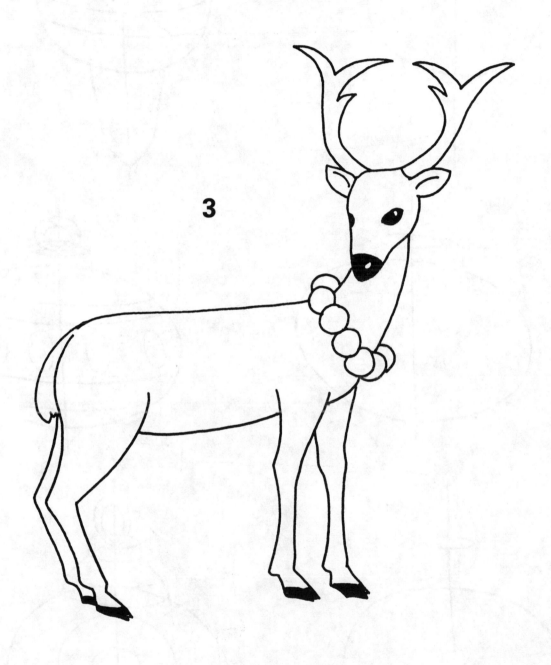

3

REINDEER

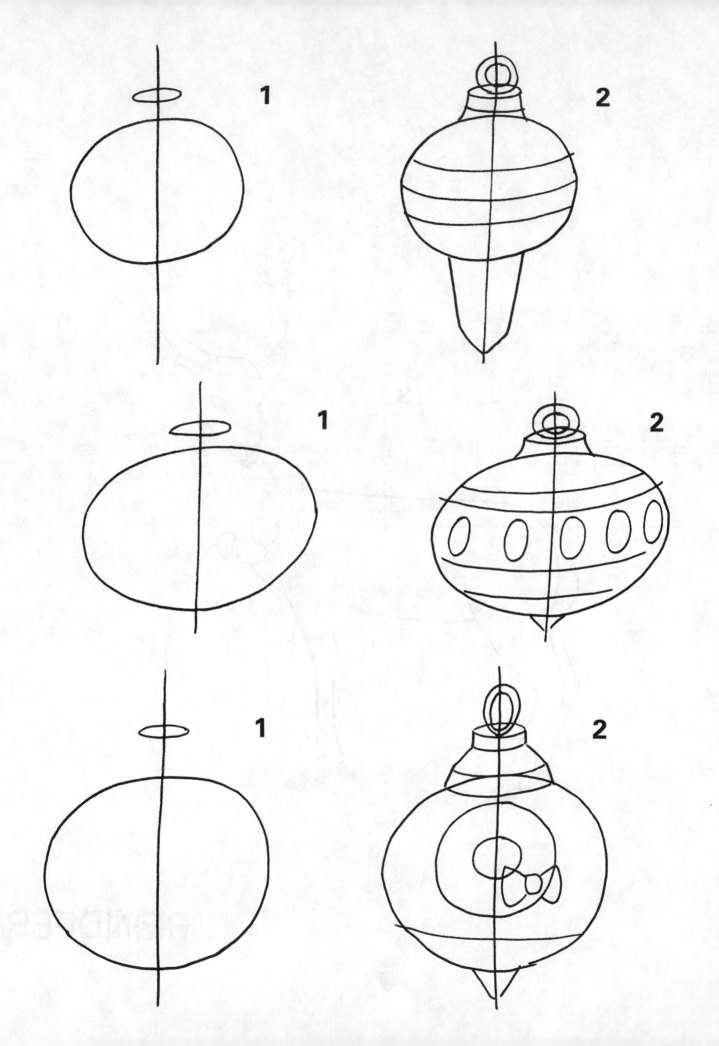

1

2

1

2

1

2

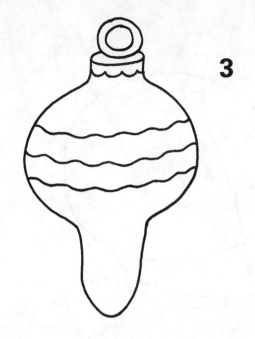

3

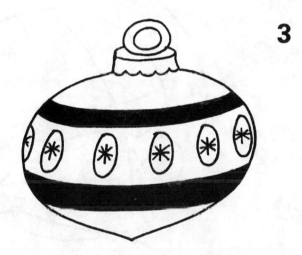

3

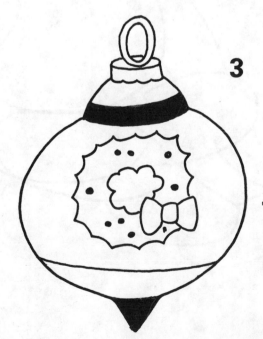

3

TREE
ORNAMENTS

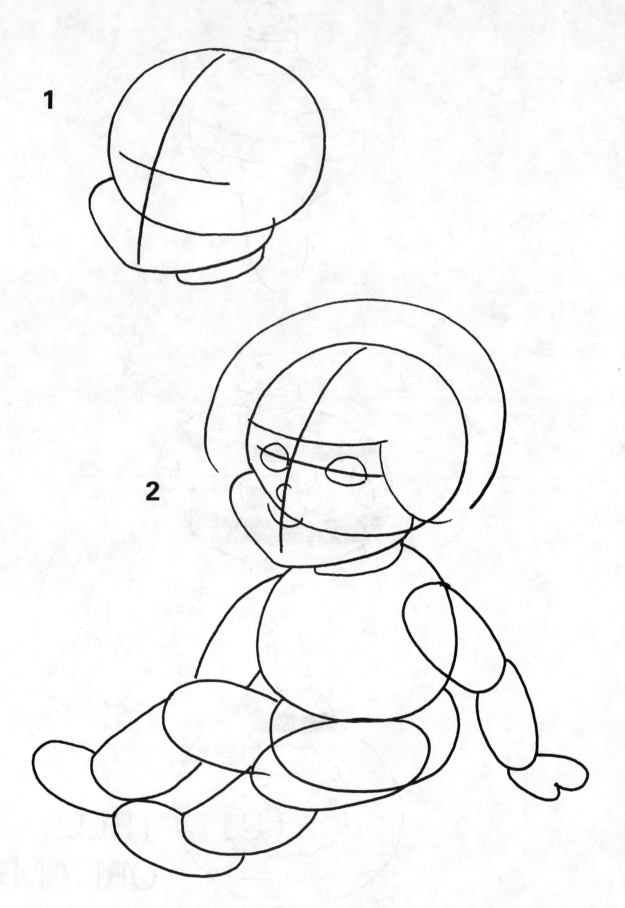

3

DOLL

1

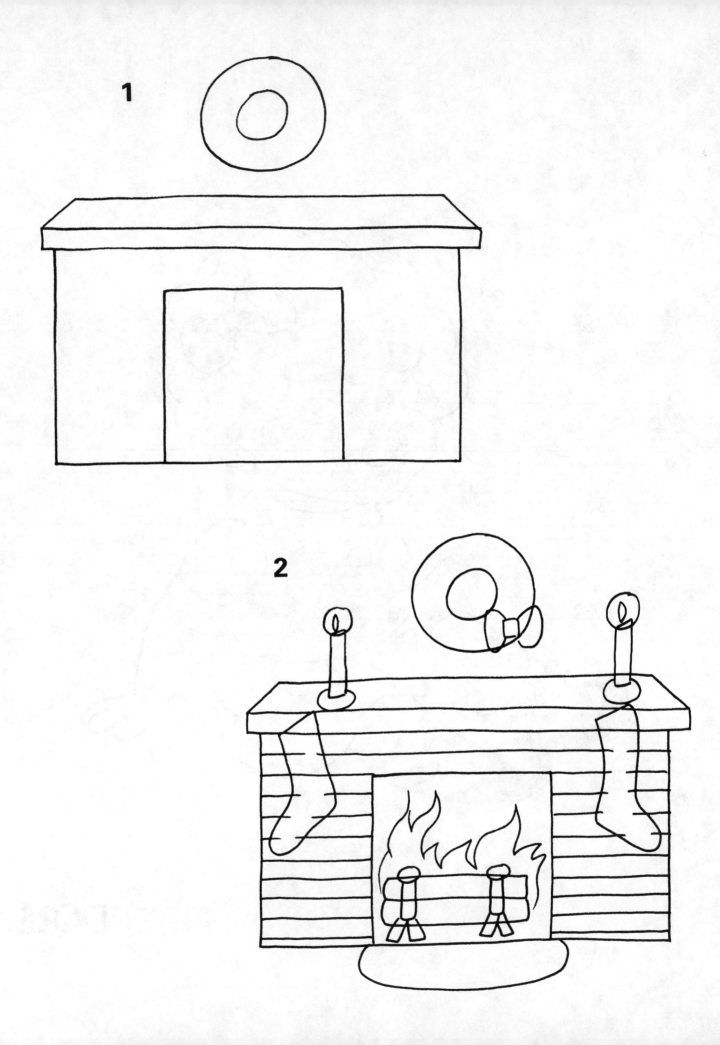

2

3

FIREPLACE

1

2

3

SANTA'S LIST

GINGERBREAD BOY

1

2

3

SNOWMAN

TEDDY BEAR

1

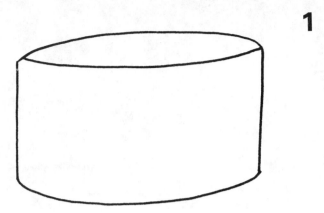

2

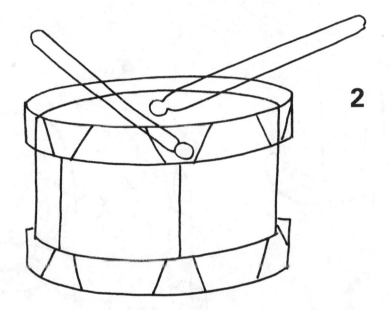

3

DRUM

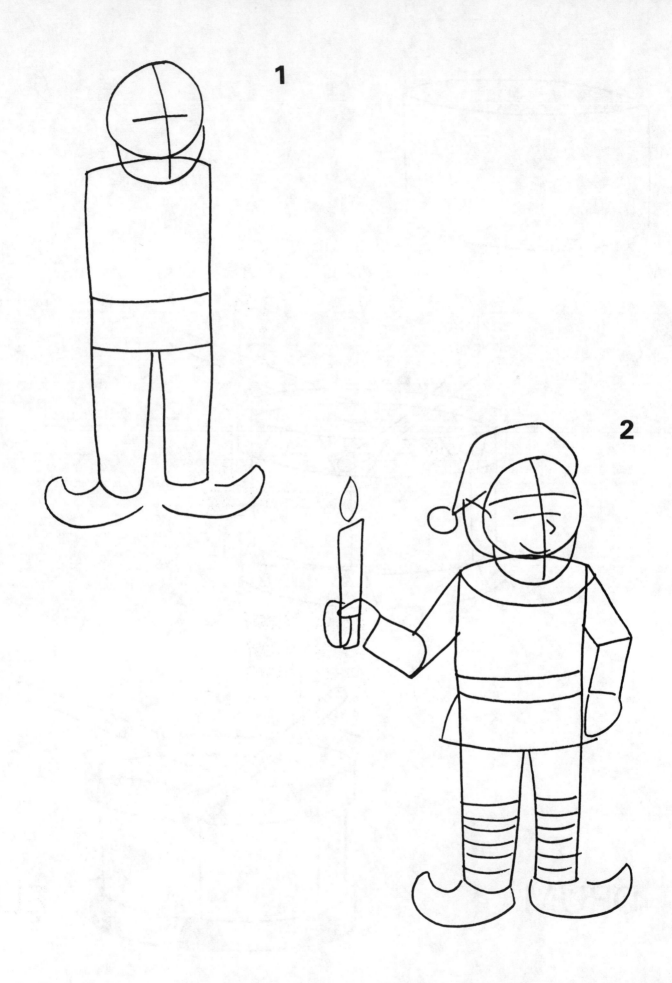

1

2

3

ELF

ROCKING HORSE

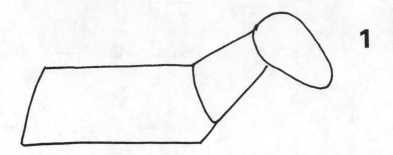

1

2

3

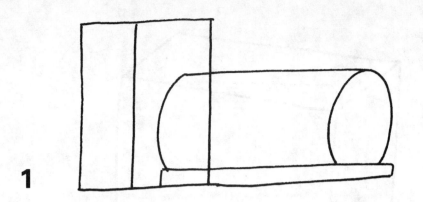

TOY
TRAIN

1

2

3

1

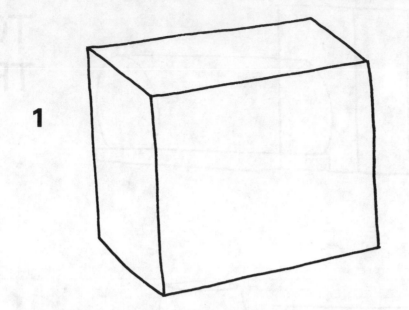

2

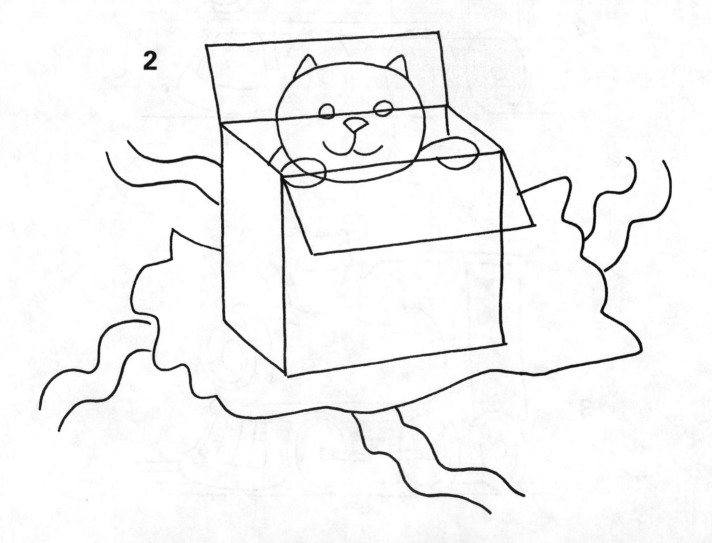

3

CHRISTMAS KITTEN

3

"HO-HO-HO!"

1

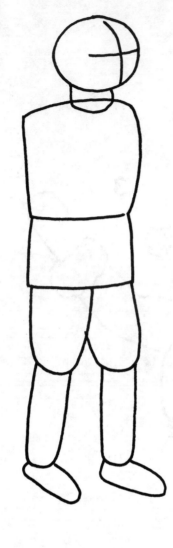

2

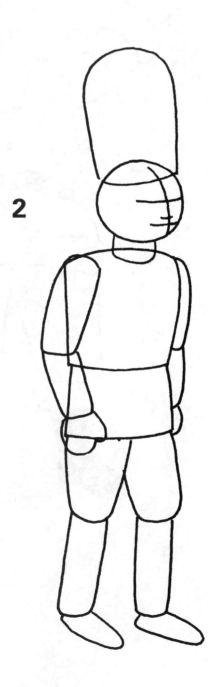

3

TOY SOLDIER

1

2

ANGEL **3**

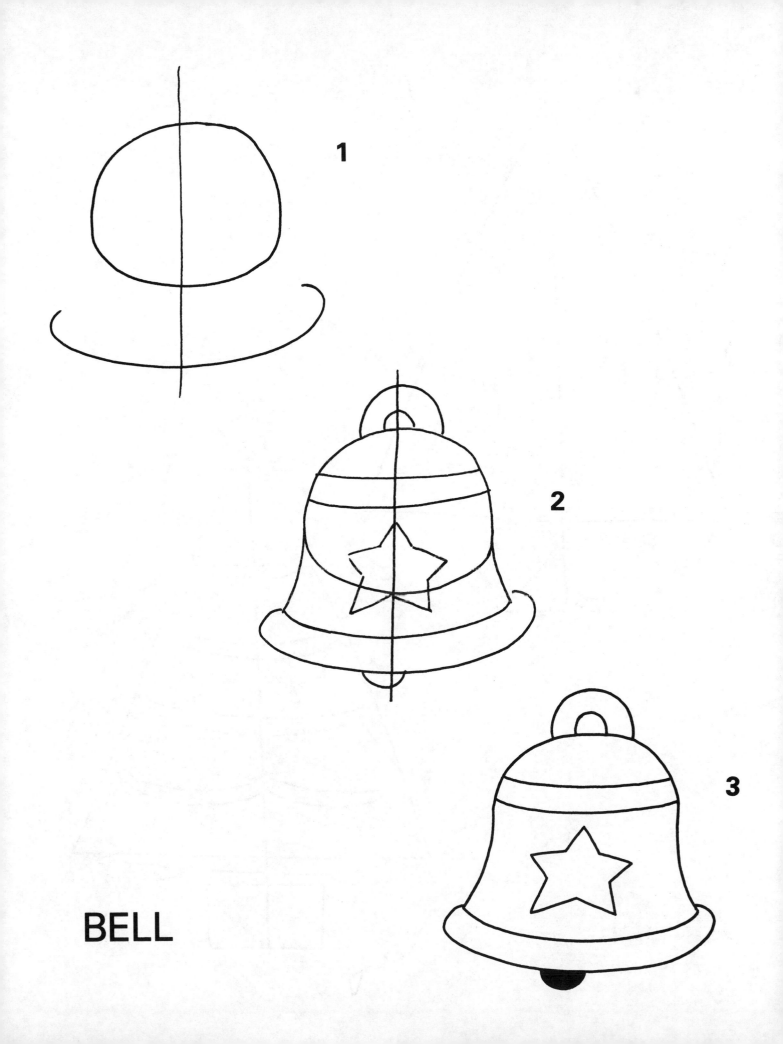

1

2

3

BELL

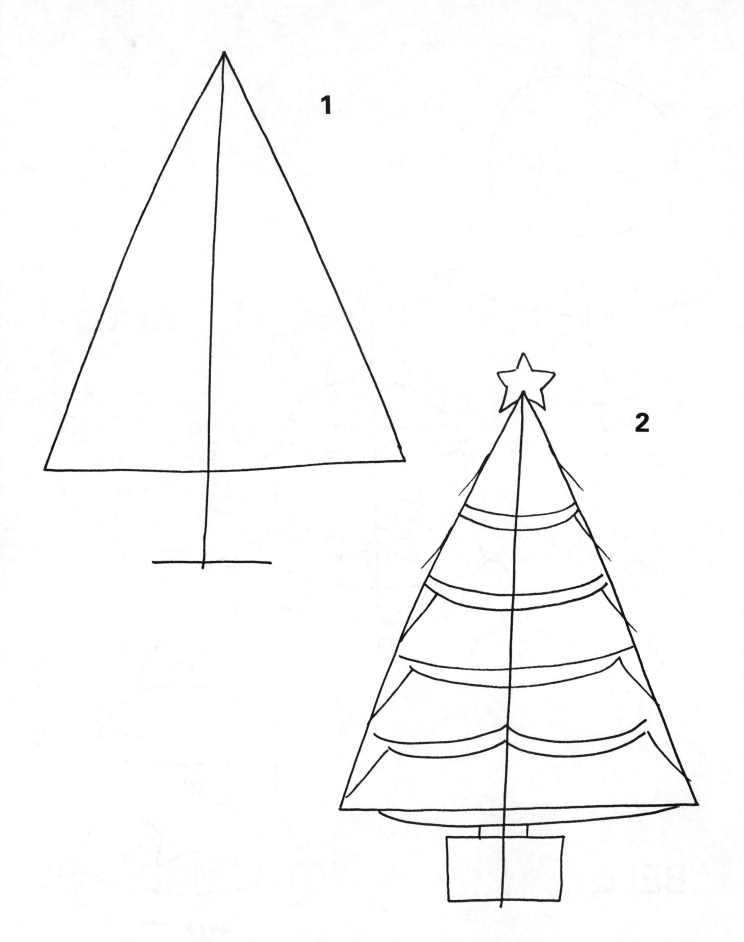

1

2

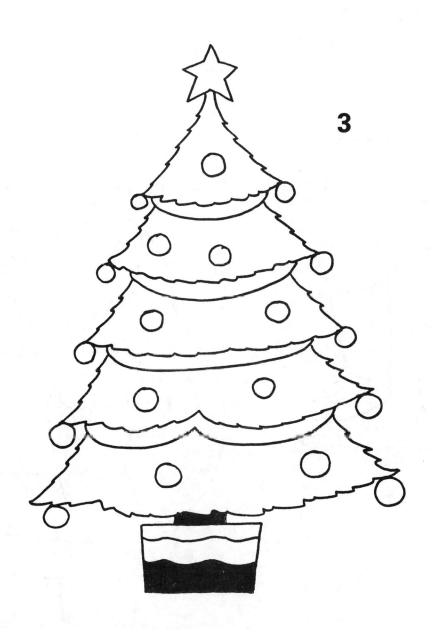

CHRISTMAS TREE

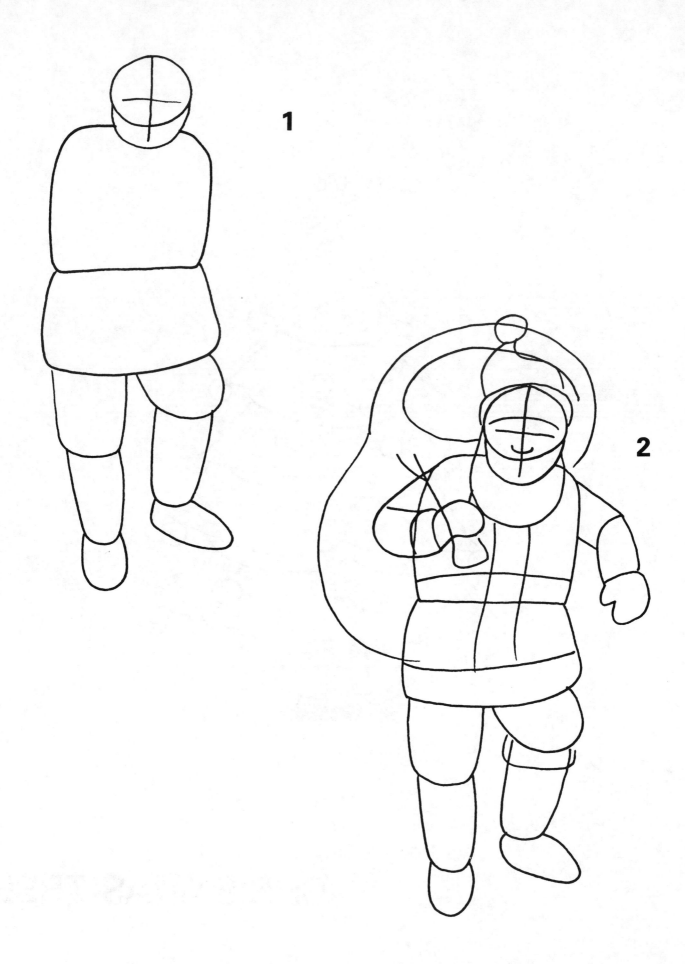

3

SANTA CLAUS

1

2

3

MRS. CLAUS

1

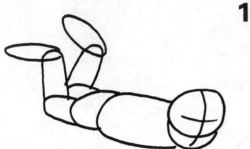

2

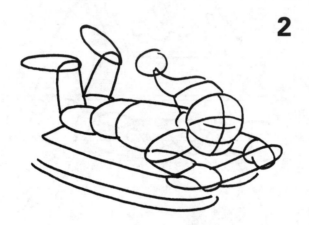

3

SLEDDING

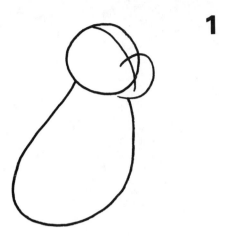

1

2

3

CHRISTMAS
MOUSE

1

2

3

THE CHRISTMAS TREE

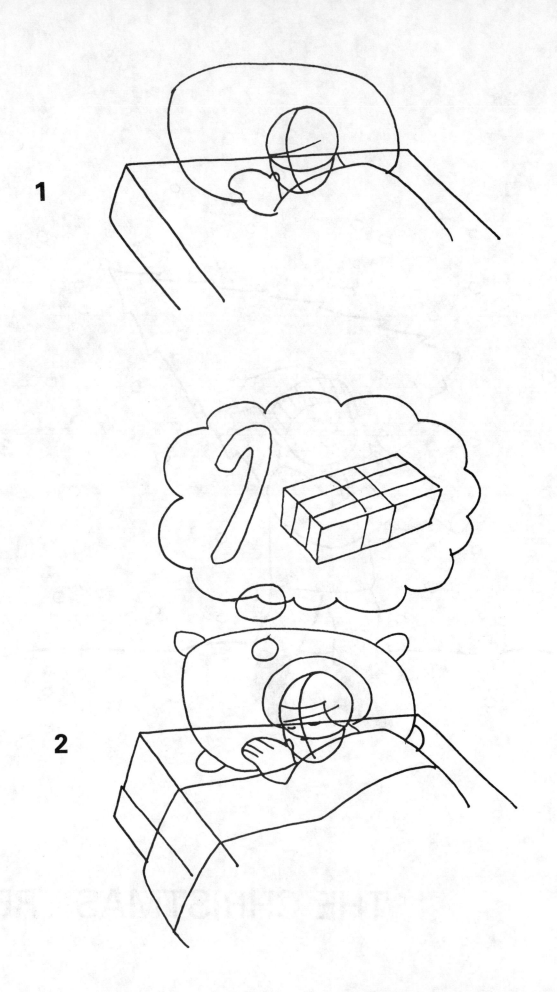

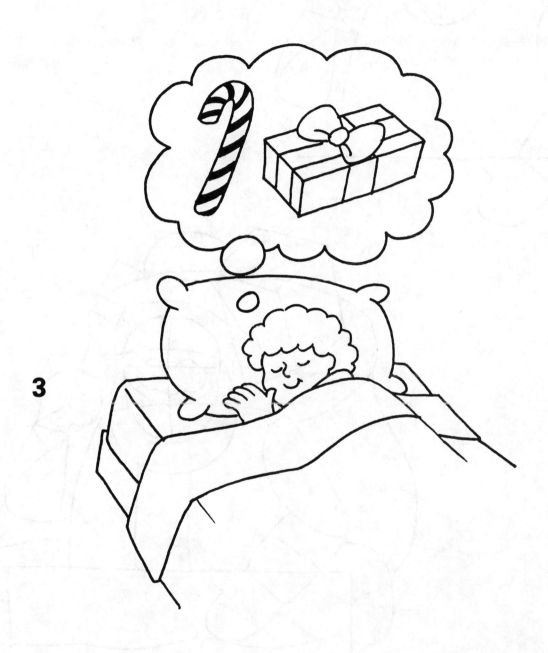

3

**CHRISTMAS
EVE DREAM**

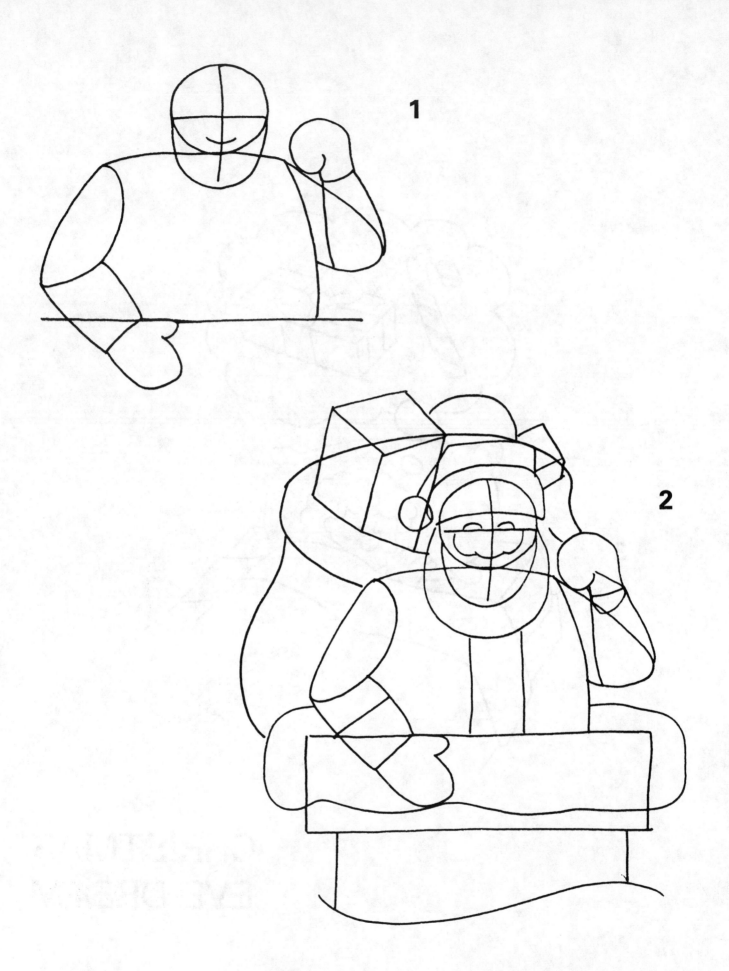

1

2

3

DOWN THE CHIMNEY

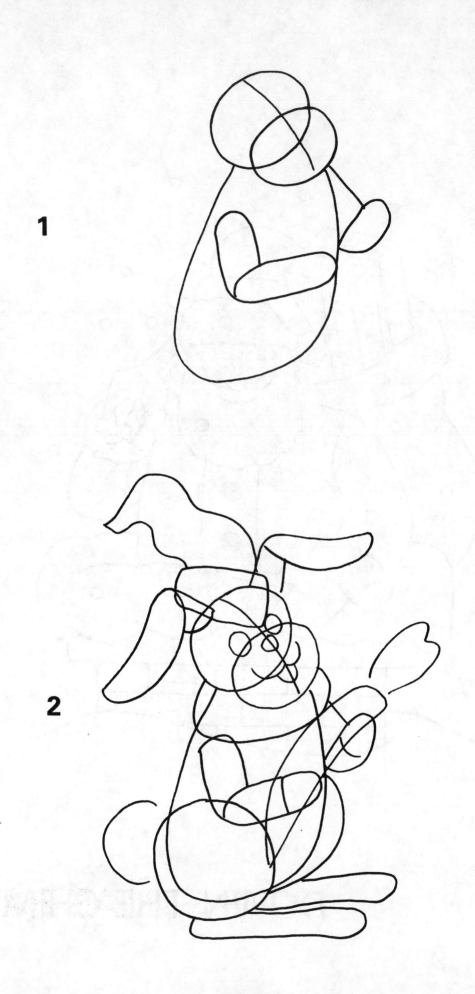

3

CHRISTMAS RABBIT

A CHRISTMAS GIFT

1

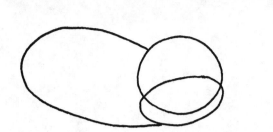

2

3

PUPPY'S GIFT

1

2

3

SCROOGE (BEFORE)

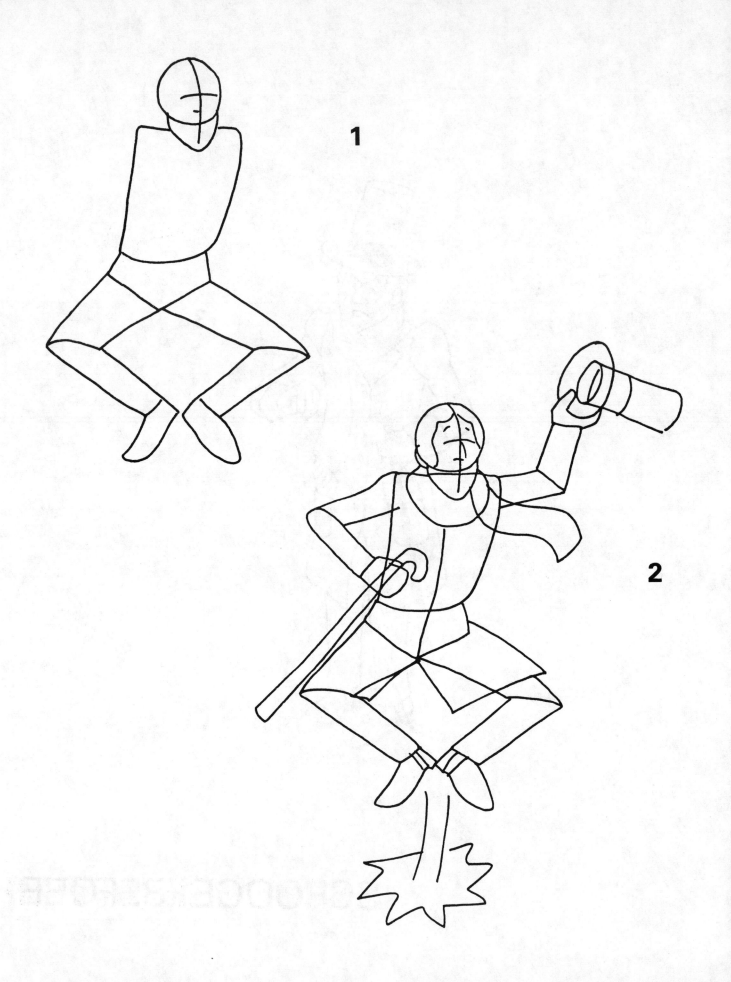

3

SCROOGE (AFTER)

1

2

3

SKIING SANTA

FLYING REINDEER

1

2

3

SNOWWOMAN

1

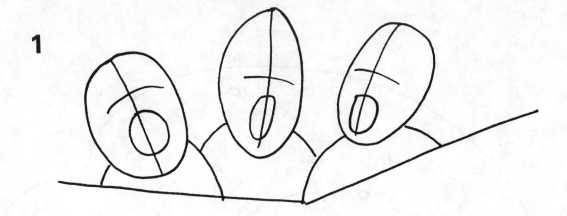

2

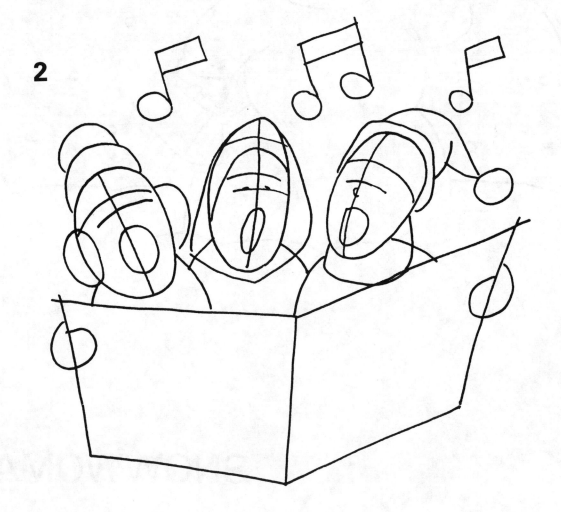

3

"DECK THE HALLS"

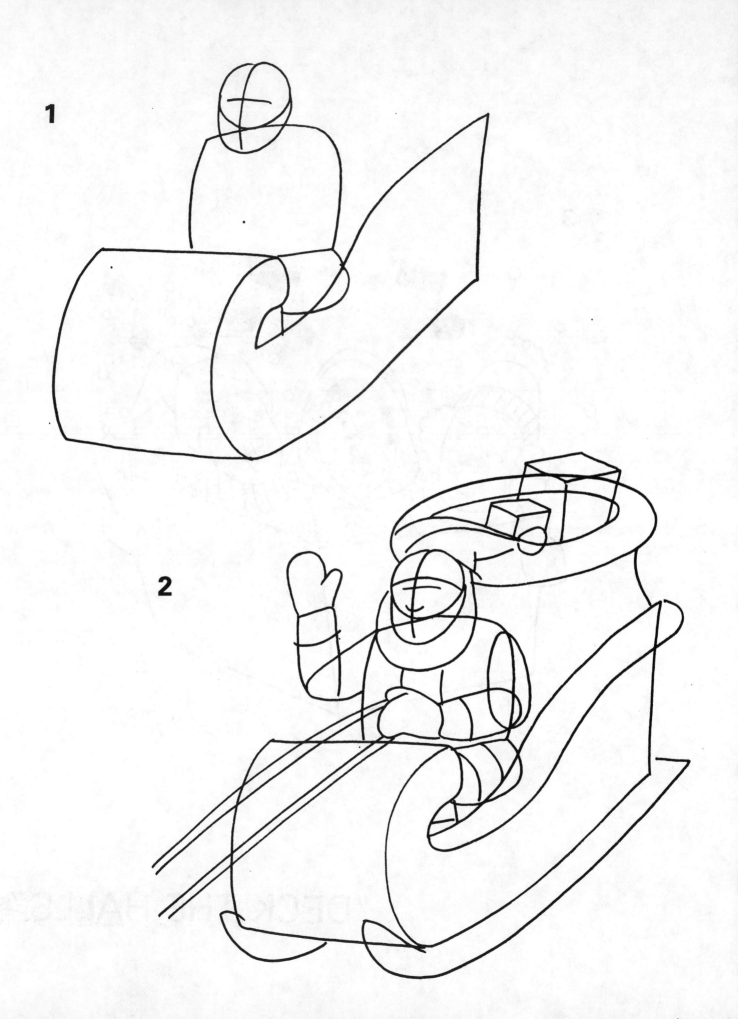

3

SANTA'S SLEIGH

1 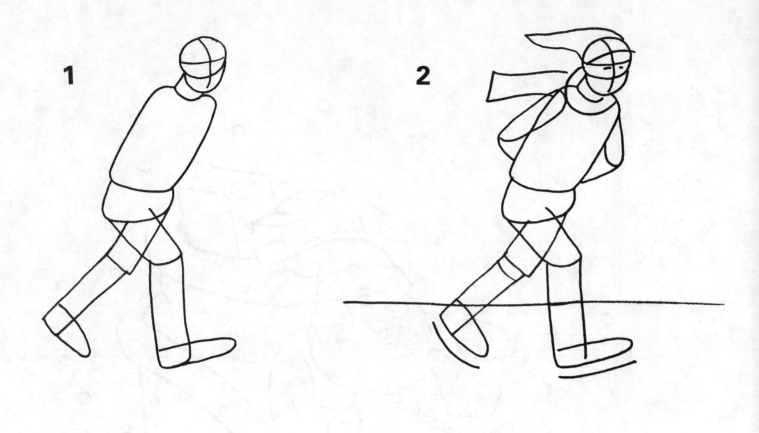 **2**

3

SKATING I

1

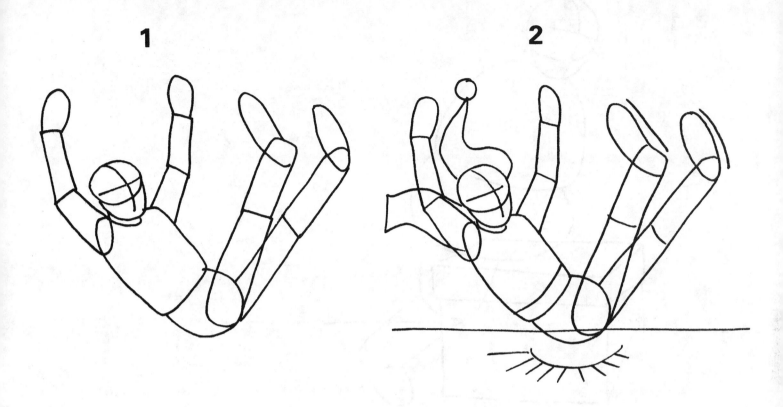

2

3

SKATING II

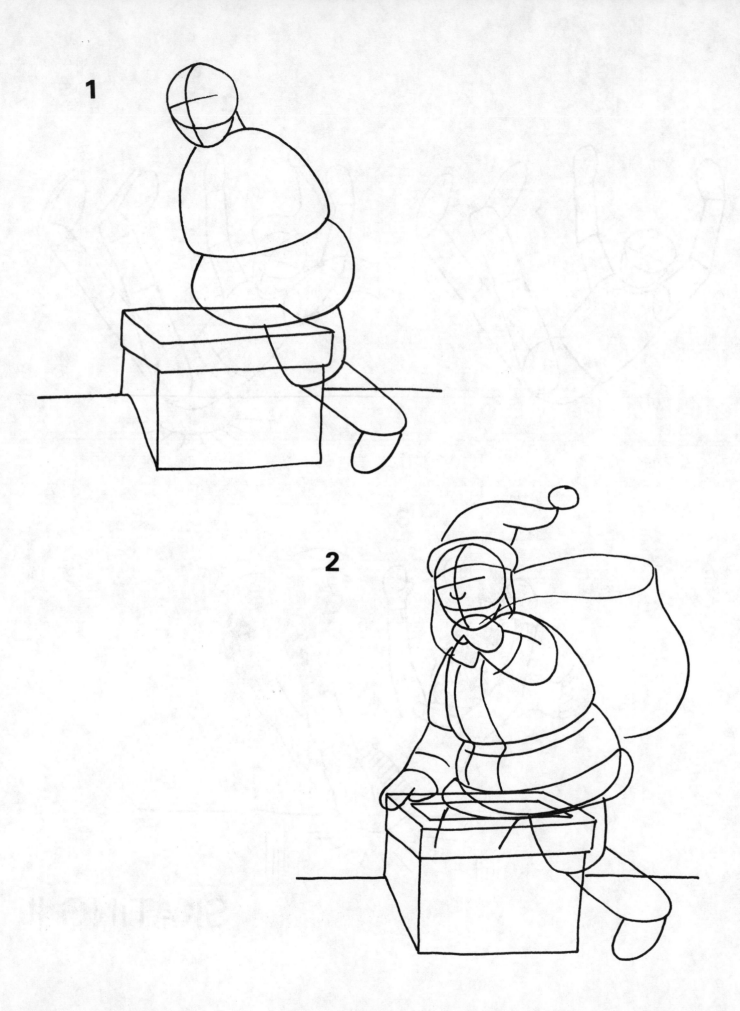

3

DOWN THE CHIMNEY

1

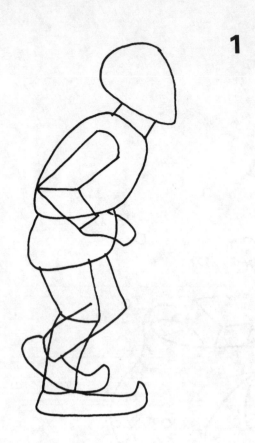

2

3

SKATING ELF

This drawing looks more difficult than it is!
Just take your time and follow all 6 steps and you can draw it.

1

2

3

SANTA AND HIS SLEIGH

4

5

6

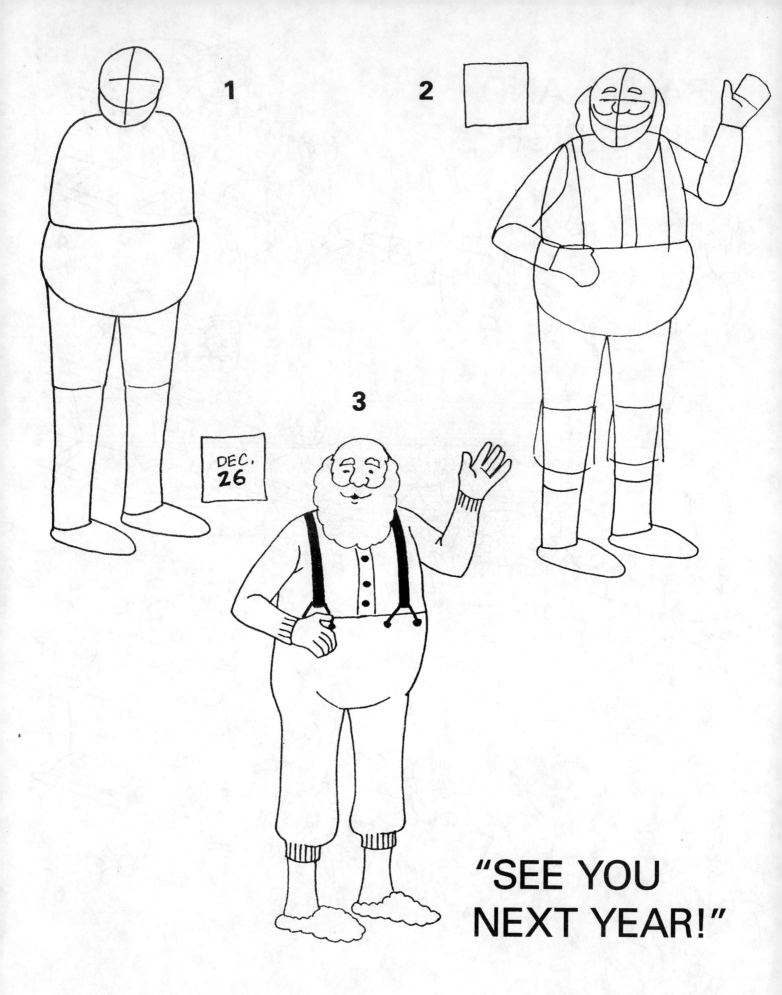